Servicetopia

The ultimate
customer service experience

by

Jason Young

This book is dedicated to those who diligently serve others.

To those who know that it takes courage, dedication, and commitment.

To those who know that customer service isn't a strategy, but rather a way of life.

Servicetopia

Copyright © 2015 by Jason Young

Published by
LeadSmart Inc.
Dallas, TX

Printed in U.S.A

Contents

Preface

How do successful companies create both high fulfillment and high performance with their employees? The key to real success for any workplace lies at the very heart and soul of the organization – it's culture. When leaders understand how to measure, define and drive company culture and take action to integrate the values and behaviors consistent with an environment of care and accountability, they will witness an emerging, motivated workforce characterized by optimism, productivity, fulfillment and innovation. When this occurs, Culturetopia has been attained. In his last book, *The Culturetopia Effect*, speaker, trainer and author Jason Young provided his insights and practical ideas on how to create Culturetopia in any organization.

In this newest book, *Servicetopia*, Jason explores how a company's customer facing workforce can deliver the ultimate service experience, where high levels of customer satisfaction and retention are sustained. Servicetopia is where employees derive personal and professional satisfaction as a reward unto itself and where the customer is the beneficiary.

If you are involved with anything that delivers value to your company's customers – face-to-face or behind the scenes – you are in customer service, and this book was written for you and for everyone who strives each day to create and live Servicetopia.

1.

The Quest

Imagine an environment where all employees are aligned with the mission and vision of the company and every day they go to work committed to providing exceptional service to every customer.

They understand their **purpose** in the organization.

They perform their duties with **passion** as they seek to meet every customer's needs.

They are **professional** and work tirelessly to build customer loyalty.

They follow a carefully outlined **process** to ensure every customer touch point is handled delicately to ensure customer satisfaction and eliminate pain and frustration.

And in the end, they add a little **pizazz** to exceed customer expectations. This launches conversations that spread to other potential customers.

This is the meaning of Servicetopia, and it can be achieved in your organization.

Customer service is a craft. As with any craft, it takes time to learn. It starts with the right attitude and commitment. Without this, your results will fall short of Servicetopia.

Learning the craft of customer service also takes place in public view. Thanks to social media, a single service encounter could be communicated to millions of consumers! Think about that the next time you consider the value of customer service training. Employees learn on the job, but without training or guidance along the way, the results could be devastating. However, with the proper tools and training even the newest employees can surprise and delight their customer!

This book will do more than tell you how to be great at customer service: it will provide you with the insights and understanding so you can create your own personalized approach to Servicetopia.

2.

PURPOSE

I'm compelled to achieve Servicetopia.

The Legend of Johnny Bagger

Johnny is a bagger at a Midwest grocery store chain. One week, the company sent Johnny along with his fellow employees to a conference about customer service. At the conference, the keynote speaker challenged everyone to "make a difference and create memories for your customers that will motivate them to come back." Johnny listened closely and took this challenge to heart. He wasn't sure that he could make a difference, but he went home with a purpose.

He wanted to follow the advice and create his own unique signature. He thought long and hard about it, then had an idea. He decided to gather inspirational quotes – a new quote for every day. With the help of his father, every night he printed out 50 copies of his thought for the day, cut them into small squares, signed his name on the back, and wrote, "Thank you for shopping in our store." When he went to work the next day, he just slipped that little piece of paper into the bag of groceries he happened to be bagging that day.

Pretty soon thereafter, the store manager noticed that Johnny's check-out line was three times longer than any other line. And, no one wanted to leave the long line for a shorter line because they all wanted to get Johnny's quote of the day.

Before long Sam, the store florist, got inspired by Johnny. Any time he created a corsage that a customer didn't claim or he discovered a flower broken off its stem, Sam would walk out into the store aisles, find a young girl, a senior citizen, a lonely shopper, and give the blossom away saying, "Thank you for shopping with us." And that inspired the butcher, Hank. Hank likes Snoopy and has a collection of Snoopy stickers. Every time he wrapped a steak or something from the deli, he would adorn the package with a Snoopy sticker. It was a chain reaction.

Create Your Service Personality

Purpose begins with you

Johnny Bagger, who was 19 years old at the time, has Down Syndrome. His story is the perfect beginning to Servicetopia. He takes his work to heart. He makes work matter. He shows appreciation. He gives his work that extra special touch. He pays it forward. And, he makes it personal, the first step toward giving purpose to your work.

So why are you in your job? Did you choose service or did service choose you? You may have made a deliberate choice to go into a service profession and work with people every day. You went to school, earned a degree or professional certification, and started your career. However, you may have landed in a service role by happenstance. That happened to me. I didn't choose training as a career; training chose me. Southwest Airlines put me in a training role, and I loved it. I wouldn't have known that until I got the opportunity to do it. To this day, I get renewed energy every time I teach because I just love doing it.

It's happened to countless others, maybe even you. Meet Christy. When she graduated from high school, she didn't plan to go to college, but wasn't quite sure what kind of career suited her. She needed a job and began working at a department store, thinking it would be fine for a while until she decided what she wanted to do. Thirty years later, she's still there, in the big and tall shop. You can tell Christy loves her job. She is always there, always helpful, always cheerful. She gives great service, suggests shirt and tie combinations, and points out the great sales. I know that I'm always going to get great service. And, I always shop there.

Not everyone is naturally good at customer service, and not everyone can be trained to become an expert. We don't expect just anyone to excel as a musician, as a brain surgeon, as a carpenter just because they have attended the right training courses. The same holds true for customer service.

Customer service happens to be in my DNA. It's just how my brain works. It's how my heart works. When I see good service, it inspires me to give good service in return. It inspires me to copy that behavior. Like it also did in Johnny's case, great service reproduces itself in the hearts and minds of other great service providers.

But what if customer service is not in your DNA, and you're in a customer-facing role. Can that work? Yes. There's more than one way to be a great service provider. Attitude, temperament, and insight all make a difference. For example, Carolyn works in the call center processing returns and replacements for a big online retail company. Some say she just punches the clock and gets on with the day.

But Carolyn has a purpose. When it comes to process she

just can't "not" do it. Carolyn cares about doing a good job accurately and quickly. When Carolyn speaks with customers, she is not overly friendly or gregarious. She has a pleasant voice; she is polite, and she's a meticulous tactician. She follows each step, guides the customer through the return, selecting a new product, or issuing the credit. One, two three, it's done, and the customer goes on their way. Carolyn gets the highest customer ratings in the house when it comes to fulfillment processing, even when the fulfillment is a return from an angry, dissatisfied customer.

Ask yourself

- Did you choose service, or did service choose you? If the situation were reversed, what, if anything, would you do differently?

- How do you describe your purpose at work?

- What is your unique service signature? What could it be?

Make connections

Customer service is personal first, then it's about relationships. It's so easy to get caught up in the transactions and forget that we are in a relationship business. Customer service is and always will be a relationship business. Building relationships with customers is no different than building friendships with your peers. Trust is established over time through reliability, availability, honesty, listening, helping, serving and kindness.

No matter what landed you in the customer service role, whether you have the DNA or not, you understand that delivering exceptional customer service involves building relationships and keeping those relationships. It's a choice.

Have you ever connected the dots between what you do and the impact it has on a customer? Whether or not you find yourself face-to-face with the customer, what you do in your line of work in some way impacts a customer. Even if you're not employed in a customer-facing role, you may work with someone who is, and, ultimately, what you do – or don't do – influences a person's decision to become a return customer.

There may be a chain of events along the way, but ultimately customer service comes down to an interpersonal transaction when the customer gains something from the product or service your deliver. The transaction could be as simple as selling a cup of coffee to an early riser or as complex as closing a multi-million dollar contract between two corporations.

Neither transaction will come to fruition unless there is, first and foremost, a positive, trusting connection between the customer and the organization, between the two people engaged in the transaction. Will the coffee be hot? Will it taste good and be reasonably priced? Can I expect the same quality product and service if I come back tomorrow? If I sign the dotted line on this multi-million dollar contract, am I confident that the people I'm dealing with are trustworthy? If I have a question or a problem down the way, will someone be available and will they be as easy to work with as they have been in the negotiation stage?

The statement "satisfaction guaranteed" is a service promise customers take seriously. If there is any doubt, any hesitation on a customer's part, there is no trust. Without trust, there is no relationship and with no relationship, the service promise is meaningless. When you think about your job in that way, your role takes on more meaning. It gives you purpose.

15

Ask Yourself

- Are you reliable when customers need something?

- Are you available when customers reach out?

- Do you provide solutions when a customer asks for help?

- Can customers count on you to keep your promises?

- Do you act with kindness in all situations with all customers?

"Your work is going to fill a large part of your life, and the only way to be truly satisfied is to do what you believe is great work."
Steven Jobs, Co-Founder, Apple, Inc.

▶ *Servicetopia Insight*

Employees only ask for the customer's name 21% of the time. Hint: The person has a name 100% of the time, and they like hearing it.[1]

Make work matter

Talk to just about anybody in the workforce, and they will tell you that they are at their happiest at work when they connect what they do with meaningful work. They know what they are being asked to do, and they see their role as important. There is also no question in their mind as to why they do what they do.

Customer service professionals who delight their customers do so by taking responsibility, not waiting for someone to give them it. They have a clear focus on delivering what is promised and recovering quickly and completely when expectations are missed. They have made giving great service to others part of their personal mission. "If I'm going to be in service, I'm going to make it matter. Scout's honor."

When the day ends and they leave the workplace behind, there is a sense of contentment knowing they have truly helped someone either directly or indirectly. Everyone likes to go home with a paycheck. Going home with a paycheck and personal satisfaction that you fulfilled your personal mission for the day – so much better.

Ask yourself

- What's your unique service personality?

- How can I start my day with purpose so I can achieve a greater sense of accomplishment?

- What difference do I make in the life of the customer?

"The ones among you who will be really happy are those who have sought and found how to serve."
Albert Schweitzer, theologian, philosopher, physician,
Nobel Peace Prize Winner, 1952

► Servicetopia Insight

"Opportunities to use skills and abilities" holds the number one spot as the driver for job satisfaction (63%). For the first time since 2007 job security was bumped out of the top spot (61%).[2]

@Culturetopia
If I'm going to be in service, I'm going to make it matter. Scout's honor #Servicetopia

Servicetopia Is a Spirit and a Practice

Spirit becomes the vision

Think about how different Johnny and Carolyn are in their personal styles. You, too, have skills and abilities that no one else possesses like you do – your own personal style. How can you bring those skills and abilities to your service role, fueled with passion, to provide great service to every customer with whom you connect? The way you do that becomes your service personality.

Every business has a personality, too, ideally grounded in a service vision that inspires each and every employee. An inspiring service vision, though, goes well beyond the decoration hanging on the wall in the corporate office or the speech made during employee orientations and annual shareholders' meetings. Great companies have a clear, actionable service mission and vision. They reward, inspire and make sure everyone understands and embraces that vision. It starts during the interview process, is defined in the early stages of employee training and development, and is reinforced every day by rewarding the right actions and behaviors of every employee.

A true service vision is a living, breathing mind set. A great service vision drives behaviors. It is through the behaviors of each individual employee that the business personality takes on its true character. There is no ambiguity in what it means. It is active and dynamic. There is nothing static about it. And, if the

company mission doesn't drive behavior that can deliver on that mission, what's the point?

Let's put these considerations into context. I worked for Southwest Airlines for 10 years. I don't remember all the individual tasks I did every day at work for those 10 years, but I do remember the promise we made to our customers stated in the Southwest Airlines vision statement:

> The vision of Southwest Airlines is dedication to the highest quality of customer service delivered with a sense of warmth, friendliness, individual pride, and company spirit.

All Southwest employees are trained on what to do in their jobs. The vision statement guides employees on how to do their jobs. With a clearly articulated and trained company vision, the employees knew how to behave, and they set a new threshold for the industry when it came to creating an exceptional travel experience. Flight crews introduced humor into the cabin. Customer service agents smiled, used the customer's name, and thanked them for flying Southwest.

The mission became the Southwest brand. It is no accident they are still recognized as a top aviation company offering outrageous customer service excellence year after year.

Discuss with your team when you get together

- What personality does your company have? Do you like that personality?

- If you have a great company personality, how can you make your company personality a part of how you treat customers every day?

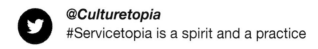

@Culturetopia
#Servicetopia is a spirit and a practice

The bank without a vision

Unless there is a strategic focus to promote and maintain a well-crafted business personality, a company could develop a negative culture that actually repels customers instead of attracting them. That was the case at the bank with no shared mission or vision.

I met some of the bank managers after my keynote speech at a banker's association convention, and they invited me to visit their company to spark some enthusiasm in their team. I was surprised to learn that this bank, 115 years serving the community, had no defined mission, no shared vision, and, to them, no real culture.

I was surprised by that. I said, "I really encourage you to develop a vision statement, because you do have a culture whether intended or not. And if you don't shape your culture it will create itself from the prevailing values, attitudes and behaviors. What do you think it is?"

From their response, it was clear the group was divided into two basic camps: the people who really cared about giving great service and the other who cared less about actually serving the customer. With that, each side had it's own service personality reflected in what their customers would experience.

One teller, Rachel, admitted that she just didn't like dealing with people anymore. What irritated her the most? This one customer who came in every day, walked up to the counter, and never had his deposit slip filled out. He expected her to do it, and it bothered her. It wasn't what she wanted to do. At

times, she would just tell him to step aside to fill out the deposit slip.

Rachel told her colleagues that her customers were being lazy. She also complained that other customers had to wait at the drive-thru window, lines building, while she filled out deposit slips.

We have a responsibility as service providers to educate the customer and let them know the best way to get great service. Since the deposit slip aggravation was impacting her ability to serve others well, Rachel had a responsibility to help educate the customer. Perhaps send out an envelope full of deposit slips to each customer and include a little note: "Please help us give you better service. Come to the service counter with your deposit slips filled out so we can serve you quickly and accurately. See you soon. Thank you."

But, we also have to realize that some people just want you to do it for them. The customer may not always be right, but they're always important.

Now back to the bank's mission and vision and the name of that bank – Home Savings Bank. If I moved to their town and asked someone on the street where I should do my banking, they should point me to the Home Savings Bank. Why? Because they feel at home there. They feel cared for when they step up to the counter. They like the people who take care of them. A shared bank mission and vision would have helped Rachel know how to behave, perhaps learn to like her job and her customers, and put purpose back in her workday.

Ask yourself

- Do your personal behaviors reflect your company's mission and vision? If not, consider why and take the necessary actions to adapt on behalf of your customers.

- What situation have you faced when a customer really irritated you, and how did you handle it? What would you do differently today?

"Loyal customers, they don't just come back, they don't simply recommend you, they insist that their friends do business with you."
Chip Bell, Founder, Chip Bell Group

 @Culturetopia
The customer is not always right, but they're always important. #Servicetopia

Uncover your service vision

As the bankers learned, businesses can serve the community or they can just make money. Or, they can make it their product to serve the community, and the by-product will be that they're all going to make money. If you're in a car dealership, if you're in a bank, if you're in a retail store, in a resort hotel, or if you're in a restaurant, it's the same principle.

Maybe your company doesn't represent great service at all, but you want to represent great service because it's who you are. So, first, check with your company. Do you have a corporate vision statement? If not, let that fly. Then, check in with your department. Would it be okay to come together and create the department's service vision? Not doable? Then, check in with yourself: "What can I do personally to create my own service vision."

The point is, no one gets off the hook. Ultimately, it comes down to the individual service provider. Identify the behaviors you need to display to truly surprise your customers, and then deliver them with pizzazz. Ultimately, you have to show up and put your unique service signature on everything you do. You will inspire people. You will surprise people. You will motivate people. And everyone will feel great. That's Servicetopia.

Ask yourself

- What is your personal service vision?

- How does your service personality reflect your company mission?

- How do you to take responsibility to create a positive customer experience?

@Culturetopia
True service visions are a living, breathing mind set. Great service visions drive behavior. #Servicetopia

The 'Platinum Rule'

We grew up with the Golden Rule: Do unto others as you would have them do unto you. We teach our children to follow the Golden Rule. When children follow this principle, we see good behavior and fewer fights. They make friends. They learn to get along. They learn to share. They learn to love. It's a great lesson at any age. It's profoundly simple. And, it's infectious.

This simple rule wraps up mission, vision, and personal style all in one. Just think about the impact it would have on you as a consumer if everybody treated you the way you want to be treated. Substitute the word "treat" with "serve"" Apply it as standard behavior yourself, and you'll observe an amazing transformation in all of your relationships. All we have to do is answer the question — how does my customer want to be served?

I call it the Platinum Rule. Serve others the way they want to be served. If you start here and take it to heart, you're already on your way to achieving Servicetopia.

"One of the deep secrets of life is that all that is really worth doing is what we do for others."
Lewis Carroll, Author

▶ *Servicetopia Insight*

70% of buying experiences are based on how the customer feels they are being treated.[3]

 @Culturetopia
Follow the Platinum Rule: Serve others the way they want to be served #Servicetopia

3.

PASSION

I have the gusto it takes.

The Pizza Guy

Whenever anyone in my neighborhood wanted pizza, we called "The Pizza Guy." I don't recall what he called his place, because we all just knew him as the pizza guy. "Call the pizza guy." We knew the phone number by heart, and he knew us all by name, by our favorite pizza style, whether we wanted double cheese or not, or if we liked his Philly cheese steaks instead of pizza. He even knew our phone numbers, which was, typically, our order number.

His voice had that New Jersey rasp, "Hey, how you doin'? Want the special with extra cheese today?" He'd been in business for years, and there just wasn't any other place any of us wanted to call in for pizza, especially when we wanted it to taste terrific, be hot when it was delivered, and have enough pepperoni on top to make three of the frozen variety. Tony, a very friendly driver, delivered it quickly, always with a smile, and a "thank you for letting us serve you today," even when we only had one dollar to tip.

One holiday we called the pizza guy, but no one answered. We thought it wasn't possible that he had gone out of business. A few weeks later, a flyer arrived in the mail. He was still open, in the same location, with the same phone number. We were ecstatic and called "the pizza guy." But, someone else answered the phone. We went from glad to sad. The nameless phone answerer wasn't cheerful or helpful. We would have welcomed a little rough rasp.

Nothing was the same, except our delivery guy, who still worked there. When he arrived with our order, the first thing he did was apologize. Clearly, whoever had purchased the restaurant made different choices about customer service – about customer loyalty. The pizza wasn't hot or good; the cheese steak didn't have the same robust flavor; they forgot the salad. The complaints continue.

It occurred to me in a flash how that delicate balance of Servicetopia can be thrown off because someone starts compromising the vision and upsets the formula for the ultimate customer service experience. The new owner just didn't have passion.

Passion Is Contagious

Take pride in your work

Passion is the fuel that drives people to excellence. It is the differentiating quality between delivering ho-hum service and the ultimate in customer service. Passion is contagious, and it spawns customer loyalty. But in today's highly competitive world, even loyalty isn't enough. We want brand evangelists — loyal followers who talk enthusiastically about our company. The catalyst that sparks a brand evangelist's passion? Extraordinary customer service delivered by employees who are passionate about customer satisfaction!

Brand evangelists are a company's dream. We all know by

now, in today's connected world, that customers who have a bad experience tell hundreds, perhaps thousands of people all about it in an instant. Enthusiastic customers who talk about their experiences with friends and can't wait to share their excitement on Facebook and Twitter – that's a far better alternative. Brand evangelists are built one experience at a time, and your individual passion and attitude make the difference in which type of evangelist your customer will be.

You know in your heart when you're giving great service. You know in your heart when you've been true to your customer or true to your co-worker. You can try to fake it when you fall short, but deep inside, you know better. Be 100% genuine, take pride in your work, and pay it forward to your co-workers and teammates, who will be compelled to be like you.

Ultimately, we achieve Servicetopia when we pour all of our passion into our performance every day, when we take pride in our pursuit of perfection. Make it who you are, not just what you do. And when you do it, do it better than anybody. Become the ultimate customer service person, and take pride in your achievement. You'll feel great. Do it consistently and often, and you might get a raise or promotion when you least expect it.

Consider this

- What do my customers expect? This is the bare minimum, and these days it's just not quite enough.

- What could I do to impress my customers? Ask this question to start the brainstorming process and come up with ways to exceed customers' expectations.

- How can I use my passion to create brand evangelists?

- What service actions will excite my customers and turn them into brand evangelists who can't wait to share their experience with their friends?

> *"Do more than is required of you."*
> General George S. Patton, United States Army

▶ *Servicetopia Insight*

Approximately one out of two people (55%) walked away from an intended purchase in the past year because of a poor customer service experience.[4]

 @Culturetopia
Make #Servicetopia who you are, not just what you do.

Project a positive attitude

Passion begins with attitude, and your attitude starts on the inside. Negative or positive, inviting or repelling, accommodating or resistant, people quickly sense attitude, and it has a tremendous effect on your ability to establish a connection with another person. Attitude is your choice. With the right frame of mind, smiles – on your face and in your voice – will be genuine, handshakes firm, and eye contact focused. Your overall body posture will be attentive and inviting. Such a mind set and physical presence communicate attention, interest and commitment to your customers, which lays the foundation for a strong and ongoing customer service relationship.

If you are angry, disgruntled, frustrated, and anxious or

generally out of sorts, external techniques are going to be difficult to fake. People can see through pasty smiles or canned expressions. If you adopt an "others first" or a "win-win" mind set, it will influence what you say and how you physically present yourself during any face to face interaction; what you say and how you sound on the phone; what you say and how you say it in a chat or email.

It does take a lot of psychological and emotional energy to consistently deliver really great service. And, we all have days when we just don't have the zest we need – or want. Take stock each day and consider your own sense of inner well-being. Become self-aware about how your attitude will affect your performance that day. If you need to, seek the guidance of a friend or co-worker to uncover how others perceive your attitude. Then, adjust accordingly, both internally and externally.

Take the initiative. Choose to project a positive attitude, and release the service passion inside. Surprise the customer; make their day. Inspire your co-workers. The more you do it, the more it becomes who you are, not what you do, and everyone feels better. That's Servicetopia.

Ask yourself

- What attitude do I bring to work each day?

- What some are ways my attitude affects my performance?

- Do I need an attitude adjustment?

- What can I do to remind myself of my core passion?

"A man without a smiling face must not open a shop."
Chinese Proverb

▶ *Servicetopia Insight*

33% of consumers say "a rude or unresponsive customer service representative" is the most likely customer
service issue to influence them to switch brands or
companies.[5]

@Culturetopia
Seize the opportunity to impress #Servicetopia

Think like a customer

Customers are the reason your organization is in business,
and "without customers, companies will die." That's a page
out of *Culturetopia, The Ultimate High Performance Workplace!* Everyone knows that happy customers spend more of
their money with your organization and tell their friends good
things about you, which brings even more business. Happy,
loyal customers are the end game, and they are the source of
your profits.

Serving their needs, surprising them with your passion
and delivering exceptional customer service moments is your
work's purpose. Customers give us endless opportunities to
share our passion, and when things go wrong, we can fix them
quickly and turn negatives into positives.

With that in mind, think like a customer.

My dentist does not work on Fridays so she took that day
out of her scheduling calendar. You're thinking, "Must be nice,"
but there was a deeper reason. She knows her patients do
not like to have their teeth done on Fridays because no one,
herself included, wants to have a sore mouth all weekend. So
Fridays are not an option. She also has clients who can't afford
to miss work for an appointment; so two days per week she

opens at 6:00 a.m. Others want to come after work, so two days per week she stays until 8:00 p.m. Not a typical health provider's schedule, but when she changed her appointment format, she was thinking like a customer. By thinking like a customer she understands that comfort and convenience are the main priorities for her customers.

What about thinking like your internal customers, your co-workers, too? When I earned a training contract with a three-shift work rotation, we could have started out holding our classes from 8:00 a.m. to 5:00 p.m. Monday through Friday. That would have great for the training team and the day shift employees.

But, what was their perspective? When we stopped to consider that, we realized that we were making some of the employees stay up all night working their shift, then come in for training at the end of their shift. We started holding some of our training sessions from 11:00 p.m. to 7:00 a.m. to match their shift schedule and fall within their normal work week. They loved us for that. The supervisors loved it, too, because they stopped paying time and a half or double time for training during the off hours.

Put yourself in your customer's shoes. You shop at retail stores, search for goods online, and are influenced to pur-chase through advertisements and a multitude of marketing messages. What influences you when you're the customer?

If you haven't had the good fortune to experience a cus-tomer service moment that was so good that you told your friends about it, here's my advice. Shop around until you do. If you don't understand the feeling a customer gets from an ex-ceptional customer service experience, it's going to be tough to think like a customer and strive to deliver at that level. Your own service experiences may not have anything to do with what your organization sells, but it has everything to do with how.

With that perspective in mind, now, what influences you as the service provider? When a customer walks away from a service experience, what memory do you want to leave in their mind? How do you want that customer to tell their "service story" to a friend or family member? As an extraordinary experience or just a mediocre one? Forget what you know about your business and think about what your customers know and don't know about you. This perspective will change the way you provide service.

Consider this

• What is one very negative service experience you have had that you would never want to give your customers?

• What is one of the best customer service experiences you have had that you would like to create for your customers?

• If you changed places with your customers, how would you feel about your product or service?

• What level of service would you expect?

"To understand the man, you must first walk a mile in his moccasins."
North American Indian Proverb

▶ *Servicetopia Insight*

80% of companies say they deliver "superior" customer service. 8% of customers think these same companies deliver "superior" customer service.[6]

@Culturetopia
Treat every customer as if they just walked into #Servicetopia

Teammates Are Customers, Too

Use your leadership influence

Projecting a positive attitude extends beyond your customers. The level of service you give to your customers will only be as good as the level of service and respect you give to your co-workers and teammates – and the level of service and respect they give to you in return.

Let's say that we're all going to the company party tonight. Everyone's going to be there. Who do you want to be around? The positive, fun, energetic people probably come to mind. Really, no one walks into a party and says, "Hey, there's that angry guy. I'll go chat with him." Or, "She's always so negative; let me go hang out with her." You don't do that at a party because you don't want to spend your social time around angry, negative people.

And, what kind of people do you like to work with? You'll probably come up with the same people you want to hang out with at the party. People who are highly performing and highly fulfilled. Positive, fun, energetic people who go above and beyond, doing all the little things that matter in service of the customer, and their co-workers.

Unfortunately, in many workplaces, we also have to work alongside angry, disgruntled, depressed, negative co-workers. Sometimes it's tough to project a positive attitude when you're surrounded by these people. You know the type. They get into the blame game, blaming co-workers, blaming the boss, blaming the customer for whatever goes wrong.

You're probably wondering how a lesson on positivity and passion could include this negativity and blaming. Life's too short for all that. And you're right. You spend more than half your waking hours at work; so make those hours count.

Think of it this way. As a front line service provider, your current reality involves giving great service. You may be a part-time barista, a temporary contract worker for a high tech company, or a full-time career professional. Whatever your situation, however long you intend to stay in your current role, take full responsibility for your choice to be there. The more responsibility you take for your current role and your current reality, the more empowered you're going to feel. And the more positive your influence is going to be.

Now use your leadership influence with those around you. You do have it. Leadership is not about title or position, it's about influence. You've adopted a positive attitude, a cornerstone of passion, and you take pride in your work. Help cultivate your attitude of caring and accountability to all your co-workers and teammates. In Servicetopia, all that pride and passion spills over into every customer interaction.

@Culturetopia
Leadership is not about title or position. It's about influence #Servicetopia

Practice the positivity rule

Try using your positive leadership influence and adopt the positivity rule. That's what we did at Ray's Heating and Air Conditioning, a family-owned and operated company that has been in business a long time. It's is a highly successful, profitable business, the largest in their metropolitan area, and has a solid reputation for great customer service and professionalism.

The technicians had fallen into the blame game when a new manager came in and changed some of their processes. There were grumbles about the changes, a lot of gossip about co-workers, and unfriendliness toward to the new manager. Everything had tipped off balance. They all felt it; none of that feeling was good, and they genuinely wanted to snap out of it. That was the first major step – willingness to change. The passion was alive, just not well.

We gathered as a team to uncover the underlying issue – the new manager was an outsider and the techs didn't want to change. What Ray's team was reminded about that day was that they were there to serve their customers, and in this case, their internal customers, their co-workers. They talked about the need for their team to come together and gain agreement on how they wanted to work together, no matter what their state of emotions. No matter what their opinion about the new processes.

I challenged Ray's team to use the positivity rule moving forward: don't say anything bad about your co-workers; don't say anything bad about the customers; be honest, but if you can't say anything nice or respectful, don't say anything at all. We also had a no gossip policy that Ray's team implemented too. Once everyone agreed on those basic rules, everybody had permission to hold each other accountable to them. It made Ray's workplace a freer place to be because everyone knew what was expected.

It helped that the new manager was quite competent, very experienced, and customer service was in his DNA. The technicians discovered that when they opened their hearts and minds to the change. It was a good day. And the passion returned, with a full commitment to serve their co-workers, serve their customers, and hold each other accountable.

Ask yourself

- How can I use my leadership influence to increase passion and positivity among my co-workers?

- How can I help my co-worker who needs an attitude adjustment?

- What basic rules do I have, or could I create, that help foster positive team play?

"A great leader's courage to fulfill his vision comes from passion, not position."
John Maxwell, American author and speaker

▶ *Servicetopia Insight*

It takes twelve positive experiences to make up for one unresolved negative experience.[7]

Feel the passion

People who are passionate about their work and adopt a positive attitude can't be anything but passionate and positive. If your heart and mind are open and available to serve others, to make people happy, to seek Servicetopia, then the possibilities are endless.

My service passion is to please people. It comes out of my heart. I want people to laugh. I want people to like me. But I know some great service providers, where the passion comes

from their mind, from the process they follow. Whatever the source of your passion, thrive on it, use it every day, and relish in the experiences if brings to you and your customers. Everyone feels great. That's Servicetopia.

Ask yourself

- Do I have the gusto it takes to achieve Servicetopia?

- If you don't have the gusto now, what will you do to get it? It's your work; make it matter.

"If you work just for money, you'll never make it, but if you love what you're doing and you always put the customer first, success will be yours."
Ray Kroc, Founder of McDonald's

▶ Servicetopia Insight

Customer profitability tends to increase over the life of a retained customer.[8]

@Culturetopia
Your purpose at work: Deliver exceptional customer service moments #Servicetopia

4.

PROFESSIONALISM

I work steadfastly to uphold the profession.

Customer Service is a Profession and an Art

Paint your canvas

Making work matter to you and those around you, finding purpose, and feeling passion in your work come from within. But the way you express those values and principles as you serve your customers and your fellow teammates, makes the difference between being an ordinary professional and a Servicetopian professional. Customer service is a profession, and it's hard work to keep Servicetopia first and foremost in your mind, even when you feel it in your heart. Servicetopia demands ultimate professionalism in every interaction.

Customer service is also an art. Doctors practice medicine. Attorneys practice law. Why is it practice? Because they are always learning and improving their art. What about you? Are you practicing customer service, that is, are you learning and growing through every interaction? Customer service is a creative process; it's the business of developing innovative solutions for customers' needs and problems. It's a study of people and how to manage them in their relationship with your company.

Although there is a strategic process at the heart of seamless, consistent service, no two people or situations are ever the same. Those who see service as an art in which one can grow, develop, and mature are the true customer service professionals.

Here's how to be a creative professional.

Tap into your intrinsic motivation. Don't wait for a better office, higher pay, or a new boss. Find the purpose in your life that motivates you to do your best work. Maybe it's learning something new, solving a challenging problem, helping someone in need. Those motivators aren't based on circumstances beyond your control. They put you in the driver's seat.

Connect your skills and personal experience to the company's mission and vision. You are not cut out of a mold. You are an individual; so bring your unique perspective and abilities to the organization like no one else can.

Learn a new skill or increase your knowledge. New skills and knowledge fuel your creative output and produce highly engaged employees.

Set challenging goals. Stretch yourself a bit. Make it a game. Keep moving the target further and further out to maintain challenge and excitement. Maybe work is boring simply because you're reaching too low or not reaching at all.

Contribute something to others. Your customers have needs. So do your co-workers.

Figure out what it takes to enrich their lives, and make it

your mission in life to make life better for them.

All employees are in customer service, regardless of the individual assignments in their department. Rise to the level of Servicetopian professional, take ownership, immerse yourself in service, and learn what it takes to leave a positive legacy with each and every customer you meet.

> *"Professional is not a label you give yourself – it's a description you hope others will apply to you."*
> David H. Maister, author

▶ *Servicetopia Insight*

Highly engaged employees are 50% more productive, 33% more profitable, and responsible for 56% higher customer loyalty scores.[9]

Make your painting leave a lasting impression

First impressions are lasting impressions. How many times have you heard that? And, that first impression, especially face-to-face, is crafted within the first minute of the interaction. So many experts have researched this phenomenon that it has become accepted as fact.

In her book *Four-Minute Sell*, Janet Elsea outlined what people pay attention to as they form their impression: appearance, facial expression, eye contact, body movement, personal space, and touch.

Albert Mehrabian, Professor Emeritus of Psychology, UCLA found in his research there are clear distinctions in the emotional signals people send. He found 55% of the emotional signals come from gestures, 38% come from the tone of the voice, and what is actually said makes up just 7%. On the phone, he found that 82% of the cues come from the tone of the voice, and the rest from the words.

Extend those emotional signals to email or chat, and you're still on the hook. In those situations, word choice becomes critical. When you use correct spelling and punctuation, and don't "scream" with caps lock turned on, you show respect for your customer. When you project a professional image in every interaction, across every channel of communication, you show that you care about your customer's question or concerns and reinforce a lasting first impression – the best kind!

You are the crafter, the artist behind your professional image, and these critical, verbal and non-verbal behaviors are completely within your control. Remember, you are the person closest to the customer and you project not just yourself, but your entire organization. How the customer reacts to you – the impression you convey – is how they react to your organization and form their impression of doing business with you.

What can you do to create a positive lasting impression?

Appearance: Step forward with your best grooming habits and attire every day.

Facial expression: Have a smile on your face and in your voice. If you're on the phone, make an extra effort with that smile.

Eye contact: Look into your customer's face, not at the floor, around the room, or at your latest text message. If you're online, don't post on Facebook while you're chatting with your customer.

Body movement: Stand Tall. Don't fidget. If you're online, try not to slouch in your chair. An erect posture keeps your voice strong and alert.

Personal space: Be approachable and walk up to the customer. But, don't stand too close – an arm's length is a good general rule. On the opposite extreme, don't shout at the customer when they're standing across the room or deep into the queue.

Touch: Hugs are nice, if you know your customer well. But don't overdo it. Otherwise, that firm, friendly handshake always does the trick when the situation calls for it.

Be completely engaged. Give 100% of your attention to the customer. Don't talk to teammates or talk on the phone while you are working with a customer.

Paying attention to these details not only leads to a happy customer, it can also lead to raises and promotions. Projecting a professional image pays.

> *"Professionalism: It's NOT the job you DO,*
> *It's HOW you DO the job."*
> *Anonymous*

▶ Servicetopia Insight

Not only do we have 5 seconds to make a good first impression; if that first impression is bad, it takes 8 subsequent positive encounters to change that person's negative opinion of you.[10]

@Culturetopia
Projecting a professional image pays with bigger tips, raises, promotions. #Servicetopia

You have a choice

Here's a fact: You'll spend a large portion of your life at work. Here's a sad fact: The majority of people are dissatisfied at work – 66 percent to be exact – as we learned from the Right Management survey cited earlier. If you are one of those dissatisfied people, connect those first two facts and ask yourself this question: "Do I want to spend the bulk of my life dissatisfied with what I'm doing?" Probably not.

Marcus Buckingham uncovered several years ago that the vast majority of people are not engaged in their work, with 19% of those admitting to being completed disengaged. Just 26% of workers consider themselves fully engaged, feeling passion for their jobs and a connection with the company. The unfortunate conclusion I come to is that most people are essentially trading hours for dollars and may even undermine the efforts of others on the team.

Unfortunately, the group that gets the most emotional attention and who takes the most energy out of everyone is that disengaged group at the bottom. This is a trap, because what gets recognized gets repeated. And in the case of the bottom twenty, that recognition comes in the form of criticism, performance improvement plans, consequences for negative behaviors, and ill feelings.

A friend of mine, who works at a chicken processing plant, thought about that imbalance on his team and tried something different. He started spending his time recognizing strong performance, positive attitudes, initiative, and creative solutions. He connected with everybody every day to reinforce the positive, and, before long, the group followed suit. They stopped wasting energy on negative thoughts, actions, and behaviors and started sharing positive reinforcement upward, downward, and sideward.

A positive work culture emerged, and his team began feeling that they were much bigger than their job of processing chickens. They invested in each other and used positive reinforcement as their guide. This group, who doesn't have the most pleasant of tasks in the processing plant, still holds the longest streak of perfect attendance in the history of the company.

Where are you on continuum of engagement, and how do you work with others? You can blame your boss, the company, or your co-workers, and at the end of the blame game, still feel dissatisfied. You can let the grumblers continue on their angry way, or you can help them rise to the top 20%, reinforcing positive behaviors.

The good news is you have a choice. Take ownership for your own performance and use your leadership influence with your teammates. Those who take ownership and get engaged with their work will view the work portion of their lives as a rewarding pursuit rather than drudgery.

Ask yourself

- Are you trading hours for dollars?

- Do you know someone who is trading hours for dollars?

- What can you share about purpose, passion, or professionalism that might help that person turn work from drudgery into a personal pursuit?

"Always treat your employees exactly as you want them to treat your best customers."
Stephen R. Covey, author

Customers Count On You

Know your product and service

The most enthusiastic customer service representatives are the ones who have thorough knowledge of their products and confidently believe that the products and services will provide value for their customers. Enthusiasm and confidence are both infectious and significant selling points when moving customers toward complete service satisfaction.

Customers count on you to be the expert. It's a mark of professionalism. The more complex your organization's offering, the deeper you need to understand it so you can help the customer make smart decisions on what to buy and how to use the products to best meet their requirements.

Learn how your product is made. Learn what improvements have been made throughout the product service history. What are the most unique uses or applications of your services that might excite your customer? If it applies, what experience do you have with your organization's products? What practical uses have you or others found? What are all the options available? How does it differ from your competitors?

When you know your product or service inside out, you can address customer concerns, handle tough questions, and solve problems more quickly and accurately. However, when you lack confidence in answering a customer's question – or give out incomplete or inaccurate information – the customer may lose confidence in you. Trust, customer satisfaction, and long-term relationships are at risk.

You can gain product or service knowledge from all the usual sources: marketing collateral, training, operations manuals, articles, other service and sales reps, your internal knowledge base, and industry associations. Your customers are also a great source of insight. Read customer testimonials. Read the complaint letters. Follow your organization's Facebook, LinkedIn, Google+ pages and follow your experts on Twitter. It might surprise you what you learn from these less formal channels.

But your service personality, your attitude, your ability to think like a customer are also part of your organization's product and service. Hone your skills. Take classes. Read other books like this, and brainstorm ideas with your teammates on how to become a better, more knowledgeable service professional. With ongoing learning, you become an expert in your profession and can deliver Servicetopian moments.

"When we studied them, excellent performers were rarely well rounded. On the contrary, they were sharp."
Donald O. Clifton, author

▶ *Servicetopia Insight*

Customers are increasingly frustrated with the level of services they experience:

- 91% because they have to contact a company multiple times for the same reason
- 90% by being put on hold for a long time
- 89% by having to repeat their issue to multiple representatives[12]

Learn, grow, and improve

The Total Quality Management process outlined many principles to help companies increase the quality of their products and services. One such principle became a mantra for many: Do it right the first time. Doing things right the first time prevents extra downstream work that is costly and time consuming. It is also good for reputation building, trust, and increasing customer loyalty.

As much wisdom as that statement contains, it could go a bit further. In the ongoing evolution of customer service, the mantra should be: Do it better the next time.

When we get comfortable with processes and procedures, we fail to look for opportunities to improve, innovate, and continue to exceed customers' expectations. Companies that continually top the list for customer service excellence learn from every customer interaction and are constantly revising their processes.

When you or your team walks away from a customer service interaction, build these questions into your routine:

1. What did we learn about this customer's wants, needs and desires?

2. What weaknesses did this customer interaction reveal about our service?

3. From what we've learned, want can I anticipate about future customers' needs?

4. What are the customer contact points that cause the most effort and frustration for our customers?

5. What can we do to reduce the effort at those contact points?

6. What tools do we have in place to track our customers' journey with our business, and what are they saying we need to do?

Doing things better the next time requires constant attention and action to make your life and your customers' life better.

"Excellent firms don't believe in excellence –
only in constant improvement and constant change."
Tom Peters, author

▶ Servicetopia Insight

86% of consumers began doing business with a competitor following a poor customer experience.[13]

 @Culturetopia
Do it right the first time. Do it better the next time #Servicetopia

Listen to feedback – then take action

Feedback is essential for running a successful business. It tells you what's working and not working, what customers like and don't like, and what areas need to be addressed to keep your efforts on track. Your customers are talking about your service to someone; so it's important to make sure you are listening to the good, the bad, and the ugly so you can address their concerns and improve your service.

Companies that make it easy for customers to offer feedback send a clear message that service excellence is a top priority. It may take several feedback methods to make an accurate assessment regarding what customers are saying so make sure you have several channels in place. Surveys, informal questionnaires and various open discussions can provide opportunities for customers to speak their minds, and they should all be part of your company's information gathering strategy.

There are many web-based tools that can be incorporated right into your website so customers always have an easy option for voicing their opinions. Obviously the key is that someone monitors those tools and responds quickly if there are issues that require a direct response.

In today's world saturated with social media, companies make a grave mistake when they turn a deaf ear to these channels. Word spreads quickly through Twitter and Facebook and unless companies respond and participate in the conversation, irreparable damage can occur in an instant.

As a service professional, you are the closest person to the customer and probably have more direct interaction with the customer than anyone else your organization. There are no shortages of learning opportunities if we are just alert to the subtle cues around us. Don't be shy about asking your customers how they feel about your products and services. Give customers the opportunity, and they will tell you what they think.

However, it's also important to listen to their feedback even when they don't realize they are giving it. Let's consider a customer call center where most of the service is provided over the phone. What is the customer saying about your service, for example, when the customer asks, "Wait, what was your name again?" Why did the customer have to ask that question? There could be one of several reasons:

- You're not speaking clearly or loud enough.

- You're talking too fast.

- Your headset is too far from your mouth.

- The customer is slightly hearing impaired.

- The customer has a short-term memory.

- You forgot to introduce yourself.

Or, what if the customer says, "Could you say that again, I missed something?"

- Your explanations were not clear.

- You talked too fast.

- Your enunciation was poor.

- The customer was not paying attention.

These questions or statements offer subtle advice – indirect feedback – on what you can do to communicate better and improve your customer interactions. Maybe your customer was hearing impaired or wasn't paying attention. But, if you hear comments like these repeatedly, a pattern unfolds and reveals something that you can address and improve the next time.

Think about your own situation

What kind of comments or questions do you hear from your customers that may offer indirect feedback regarding service efforts? Listen carefully, talk about them, and use the feedback to improve.

Discuss this with your manager and teammates

- How are we measuring customer satisfaction?

- What channels are we monitoring that give us the best representation of what customers are saying about our service?

- How is the information we gather from these channels influencing our strategies and efforts to improve our service?

- Let's share what we know and discuss ideas to take action on what our customers are saying so we can improve our service.

"Knowing what's being said about your company online allows you to see where you're succeeding and where you need improvement."
Gail Goodman, business leader and author

▶ Servicetopia Insight

24% of American adults have posted comments or reviews online about the product or services they buy.[14]

Sometimes things go wrong

Sometimes things go wrong, and when they do, look out for your reaction. These are the times that test your commitment to professionalism. When you're facing an irate customer because something went wrong, that is the ultimate test of your professionalism. Poise, composure, keeping cool under pressure. That's the order for the moment when things go wrong.

In the airline industry things go wrong often. Weather delays. Mechanical delays. Lost baggage. Cancelled flights. Some customers go with the flow, recognizing that some of these things are simply out of everyone's control. Many customers get irate. Gate agents get stressed out. No one is really happy. During these times, it is their job to keep the people tension low.

You could be a server facing impatient diners when the kitchen gets in the weeds, a barista looking down a long line of guests when your teammate didn't show up for work, a customer service rep talking to a very angry co-worker facing a looming deadline who can't get on the network because the server is down.

Things go wrong. Apologize gracefully, and calmly, on behalf of your organization, even if it's not your fault. Recognize the problem, empathize, listen closely, and verify what you heard. If you're face to face, observe the customer's behavior. Then, fix it – quickly and completely. This is a sneak peek into the next chapter on process!

Brainstorm with your teammates

- What are the most common things that go wrong when you are working with your customers?

- Share the last customer interaction you had when you really needed to keep your cool – or you lost your cool – and help others learn from that experience.

"Every contact we have with customers influences whether or not they'll come back. We have to be great every time, or we'll lose them."
Kevin Stirtz, author

▶ Servicetopia Insight

70% of customers will do business with you again if you resolve their complaints.[15]

 @Culturetopia
Treat any problem that arises as an opportunity to do great things for the customer #Servicetopia

It's Still About Relationships

Customers take "Satisfaction guaranteed" to heart

Customer service is and always will be a relationship business. Building relationships with customers is no different than building friendships with your peers. Trust, the cornerstone of relationships, is established through reliability, availability, honesty, listening, helping, and kindness. The statement "satisfaction guaranteed" is a service promise that customers take seriously. If there is any doubt, any hesitation on a customer's part, there is no trust. Without trust, there is no relationship, and with no relationship, the service promise is meaningless.

Ask yourself

- Are you reliable when customers need something?

- Do you actively listen when customers speak?

- Do you provide solutions when a customer asks for help?

- Can customers count on you to keep your promises?

- Do you act with kindness in all situations?

"Know what your customers want most and what your company does best. Focus on where those two meet."
Kevin Stirtz, author

Walk backwards through the process

The goal of Servicetopia – ultimate customer service – is complete customer satisfaction and loyalty. One important aspect of achieving that end is the level of effort a customer must expend to have their needs met. The more effort they expend, the more frustrated they become with the process and the more dissatisfied they are with the service. Some organizations are now including the Customer Effort Score in their customer satisfaction surveys to better understand the customer experience and predict the likelihood of increased loyalty.

True improvement can materialize when you walk backwards through your customer service process and identify those areas that generate the most effort for your customers. An analysis of customer satisfaction reveals that customer effort increases when:

- Issues don't get resolved the first time

- It's difficult to reach a service representative

- Employees lack helpful knowledge

- Employees are not empowered to make decisions

- Companies don't offer the service customers need

- Products and services are lacking in quality

Now as you walk back through your customer service process, ask these questions:

1. Where will the above issues be addressed?

2. What changes need to be made to reduce the effort customers must expend?

3. What training needs to be provided to equip employees to reduce customer effort?

4. What tools do we have in place to monitor customer effort and frustration?

Knowledgeable employees, first contact satisfaction, and quick answers to questions are the most important aspects of the service experience according to the 2013 Convergys Customer Scorecard Research. It's about making things easy. But, making things easy for your customers does not happen automatically.

It bears repeating. As a service professional you are the closest person to the customer and have the most direct interactions. That puts you in a unique position to uncover ways to reduce customer effort, streamline your cost, and increase customer loyalty. Step up and offer creative solutions. That's what a highly engaged service professional can, and will do.

Consider this

- Add Customer Effort Score to customer conversations or surveys to uncover how easy – or difficult – it is to get great customer service from your organization.

"When customers have to expend more effort than they expect, they leave. High effort equals low customer loyalty."

Jim Tincher, author

► Servicetopia Insight

The top four reasons customers become dissatisfied are: repeating myself (38%), calling multiple times on the same issue (37%), too much time to resolve the issue (35%) and unempowered reps (31%).[16]

Professional rules to live by

Let's take a little detour into psychology with some helpful insight that can guide your interactions with customers and co-workers from Jody Hoffer Gittell, executive director of the Relational Coordination Research Collaborative. Jody identified two types of tension that exist every day, task tension and people tension. If you have high people tension, you are going to have low task tension, and it's going to be very hard to stay focused on giving great service. If you have low people tension, great customer service follows.

People tension can arise from interactions with negative co-workers, co-workers not carrying their load, a micro-managing supervisor, a marketing department that springs last minute sales or campaigns. These things happen, and there's a direct correlation. The higher the personal tension, the higher the potential for being distracted from task tension or great customer service: unprofessional reactions to teammates, mistakes, incorrect information, missed deadlines, and poor performance.

Evaluate the opportunities to remove the tension. Part of your job is to keep people tension low. Is there anything that is distracting you, or your teammates, from giving consistently great service? Is there a policy? A procedure? If you have a situation that is creating people tension, get a supervisor on the phone; ask for help.

The same dynamics are true with customers. If you can keep tension with the customer low, you will have a much higher probability that your customer's service experience will be positive. The higher the people tension, the higher the potential for poor customer service or a poor customer interaction. Consider the Customer Effort Score approach, which helps reveal whether or not your customer felt high tension or low tension. What could you do to reduce customer tension to improve your score?

Remember Rachel at the Home Savings Bank. She really didn't have anything nice to say about her customers. She even admitted to not liking people anymore. Her attitude and behavior created plenty of tension with those around her. Well, what would happen if Rachel just quit talking badly about the customer? Remember Ray's technicians who kept talking behind the back of their new manager and grumbling about the changes. Remember what happened when they stopped gossiping? They found the workplace to be much more enjoyable and positive.

Try putting some good rules into place, rules that everyone has to follow – no matter what. Keep people tension low, your personal professionalism high, and stay focused on delivering ultimate customer service. Try these:

- Don't talk badly about your coworkers.

- Don't mock your customers.

- Don't talk badly about your boss.

- Don't gossip.

- Don't wait for approval. Seek creative solutions for your customer.

- Don't grumble about the process. Make suggestions to improve it.

- Remember the positivity rule? Follow it.

- Make someone else's day; it makes your day great, too.

- Follow the Platinum and live by the Golden Rule.

Teamwork is what really drives performance. Recognizing task tension and people tension is the concept that reinforces the point: everyone in the organization, customer-facing or otherwise, influences customer satisfaction and loyalty. Everyone is in customer service. You spend half of your awake life at work, it ought to be place you enjoy going every day, where there is high performance and high fulfillment. That's Culturetopia, and Servicetopia thrives there.

Consider this

- Describe the last time you experienced high people tension? How did you react at the time and what could you do differently today?

- What new policy would help your team remove tension and help you serve your customers better?

- Who within your organization exemplifies professionalism, and what qualities and behaviors does that person project?

"Quality in a service or product is not what you put into it. It is what the client or customer gets out of it."
Peter F. Drucker, American Educator and Writer

@Culturetopia
Work should be for personal high performance & high fulfillment, not for trading hours for dollars #Servicetopia

5.

PROCESS

I practice my craft to perfection every day.

The Broken Shoe

Nordstrom truly sets the bar when it comes to customer satisfaction and customer loyalty. And this shows up best when they have the opportunity to turn a very unhappy customer back into the happy, loyal customer they were before they had a problem. I watched this in action one afternoon in the shoe department. I didn't know the back story, but I was so impressed with what I observed, that I had to ask Ron, the sales associate, to share the details after it was all over. And, it was all over in less than 3 minutes.

Maria has been buying shoes at Nordstrom for her entire adult life. She bought a pair of spiked heeled sandals for the Boys and Girls Club Gala, an event she co-hosted. Halfway through the gala, the heel broke off the left shoe, and she had to continue the festivities in her long, beaded gown with bare feet. Maria was hunting for bear when she arrived in the shoe department the next day to get her money back.

Ron saw Maria bustling down the center aisle of the store, shoe bag in hand, and read the signals. "Annoyed" was not the word for her mood that morning. Ron walked confidently up to Maria, reached for the box of shoes in hand, and said, "Hello, as he opened the box to see her name on the charge slip and said, "Maria, would you like me to give you another pair of shoes, or would you like a refund?" Ron completed the transaction really quickly, handed Maria the credit slip and gave her a free merchandise coupon. "Maria, please visit the hosiery department to select something else. Thank you for letting me serve you today, Maria. It's always my pleasure to serve you."

Maria knew from experience that Ron would handle the situation with finesse, courtesy, and respect; although she was irritated. She still shops for shoes with Ron at Nordstrom.

Process Has a Purpose

Every organization has processes and policies for engaging with the customer, for hiring and training new employees, for rolling out new tools, for securing merchandise, for just about every business function. These processes guide employees how to work together, and they guide you how to interact with customers.

Have you ever returned merchandise at one of the large home improvement stores? They put a process and system in place to make it easy to do business with them. And it is easy: I walk up to the customer service return center. They ask the simple question, "is it broken," or did you change your mind," so the cashier knows whether to put the item back into inventory or to return it to the manufacturer. If I have the receipt, they scan for the item and issue the credit in the same form I made the payment. If I don't have the receipt, no questions asked; they issue a store credit. They take the merchandise, and I'm on my way. No hassle.

That's why processes exist: to ensure a consistent customer experience no matter what. They are deliberate efforts to be sure that whatever the customer situation, no matter which employee serves the customer, the experience is the same high quality every time.

At Chick-fil-A, every server closes the transaction by saying, "It's my pleasure," not "thanks," or "no problem," or "next person." At Starbuck's they personalize the service by asking for your name. When your latte is ready, they say "Jason, your latte is ready," not "Latte," or "Here," or worse yet, just place it on the counter and wait for me to come. This is part of their customer service process.

Now consider Amazon.com. They've been in the top position in the Customer Service Hall of Fame for five straight years. And, the vast majority of the time, it's your iPad, Kindle, smartphone, or laptop and your credit card that is communicating with Amazon. It's all about process, delivering on commitments, and promptly fixing things that go wrong.

As with any process, there is a certain amount of flexibility built in so you can adapt the service to meet the given situation and keep the focus on the customer. Let your service personality shine, and create your own style for serving the customer with the framework you have in place. My service desire comes out of my heart. I want to please people. I want people to laugh. I want people to like me.

I know some great customer service professionals whose greatness comes from their mind, not their heart. One reason my colleagues are great is because they use the processes in place and follow them precisely to make sure that the customer's requirements are taken care of in Servicetopian style.

We met Carolyn earlier, a purposeful call center professional who had the highest customer service ratings on the team.

That's because she executed process with precision, professionalism, and promptness every time. She was reliable and kept the customer's interests in mind. Process has a purpose.

Ask yourself

- What's your own personal process for delivering ultimate customer service?

- What's your attitude about your organization's policies and procedures?
  - Do they help you?
  - Do they get in your way?

- If you don't like the processes, do you just buck the system, or do you try to make them better?

Consider this

- Be part of the solution. Think of one great suggestion to improve your process and enhance the customer experience. Then, share it with your supervisor today.

@Culturetopia
Good process has a purpose. Ensure a consistent customer experience no matter what! #Servicetopia

Customer Service Is a Craft

Study it

Customer service is a craft. It takes time to learn it, because there is a lot to learn. You can attend training classes to learn myriad of skills you need to master, the psychology of customer behaviors you need to understand, the processes you need to follow and adapt to a given situation, and the nuances of team play. During training you learn your processes, policies, and practices – the foundations of becoming the ultimate customer service professional.

After training, however, you develop the finesse and demonstrate mastery in full public view, right in front of the customer, not in a quiet workshop or laboratory. Study your craft whenever you visit a restaurant, retail store, bank, movie theater, library, law office, or any other establishment vying for your business. Take the first step in your customer service education by observing, evaluating, and learning how you were served as the customer. Then, apply that learning to your job as a service provider.

Observe. How were you greeted? What impression did you form in the first few minutes of contact with either the sales or service rep or the facility itself? What attempt was made to assess your needs, answer your questions or direct you to the right person or place where you needs will be met? If there were other customers present, what were their reactions? Were all treated equally or were some ignored? Take it all in and then upon reflection, evaluate.

Evaluate. Were your needs met, questions answered, or products and services provided? Was it a pleasant experience or did you leave frustrated? Are you eager to return or did it leave you angry, frustrated or indifferent? Were your expectations met? Were the conversations informative, rushed, rude, short or truly helpful? Most of us evaluate and assess a customer service experience whether we realize it or not. After you evaluate your experience, learn.

Learn. What were the most positive attitudes and action expressed during your experience? What do you think should have been done to impress you with their service? What do you think were the biggest mistakes made by the employees during your visit? What words or expressions were used to make it a positive or negative experience? Now, take it one step further and apply your personal experience to your customers.

Apply

Based on your experience, what were one or two lessons you can apply to your own customer service responsibilities? What attitudes or actions should you avoid based on what you witnessed? If this business asked for feedback regarding its service, what would you say and what suggestions would you offer for improvement?

"If you do build a great experience, customers tell each other about that. Word of mouth is very powerful."
Jeff Bezos, CEO, Amazon.com

▶ *Servicetopia Insight*

2014 Customer Service Hall of Fame [17]
1. Amazon.com
2. Hilton Worldwide
3. Marriott International
4. Chick-fil-A
5. American Express

@Culturetopia
Customer service is a craft. Hone your skills & follow the process #Servicetopia

Master the fundamentals

Questioning skills. Listening skills. Showing common courtesy and respect. Showing appreciation. You need these fundamental skills and attitudes so that you're ready to address the changing situations and work carefully through your organization's service process. Whether you're face-to-face, on the telephone, chatting in your company portal, or exchanging email, these skills come into play. They apply anywhere, in any situation – selling a cup of coffee, making an appointment with a healthcare provider, handling a merchandise return online or face-to-face, resolving a complex technical problem over the telephone, helping a new teammate get up to speed, calming chaos at an accident site. Practice and improve with each new situation.

Communication comes first

Building customer relationships takes time, and it takes good two-way communication, which involves asking questions and actively listening to the answers. Use questions to understand your customer, to uncover what they want, and to learn how to provide the ultimate customer service experience.

You've heard all about the different question types – probing questions, open and closed-ended questions, clarifying questions. Customers will actually tell you how you can make them a satisfied and loyal customer. All you have to do is ask – and listen. The time you spend listening to your customers could be the most valuable aspect of your customer relationships.

When you develop your listening skills you not only strengthen the connections you make with customers, but you open the door for opportunities to far exceed their expectations. A word of caution here, though. Listening and hearing are two different things. Hearing is a physical ability; listening is a skill. Hearing is also a passive activity. Listening is a decidedly active engagement. Listening involves processing, understanding, and learning. Hearing without listening means you just remain quiet when a customer speaks so as to avoid appearing rude. However, hearing without listening is rude and represents a lost opportunity to strengthen a bond between you and your customer.

Listen beyond words

Listening skills involve your eyes as well as your ears. Not everything that is "spoken" in a conversation is expressed through words. We know that body language communicates more than our words when we speak. When you listen to your customers, make sure you listen to those non-verbal cues as well. Listen to their eyes, hopefully they aren't rolling them. Listen to their face, whether they smile grimace, or frown. Listen to their hands, hopefully they're not clenched, and body position.

If you're not face-to-face, it's even more critical to use good questioning techniques and listen very closely to the words, the inflection of the voice, the cadence of the conversation. Listen beyond words to understand the full story.

> *"There's a big difference between showing interest and really taking interest."*
> Michael P. Nichols, The Lost Art of Listening

▶ *Servicetopia Insight*

> 93% of communication effectiveness is determined by nonverbal cues.[18]

Show common courtesy and respect

We live in a harried world. People are busy, rushed, annoyed, frustrated, and desperate at times. Walk through a terminal at a busy airport and you will see this first hand in concentrated masses. People are coming or going, for business, pleasure, celebration, or tragedy. On a typical day people arrive late, stand in lengthy security lines, face weather delays, equipment failures, cancelled, crowded or overbooked flights. While waiting for a connecting flight, they are on the phone regarding business deals, upcoming meetings, a family crisis occurring a thousand miles away, on their way to a graduation, wedding, funeral or the bedside of a dying loved one.

When customers walk up to a gate agent feeling concern about the flight arrangements – will it be on time, is everything in order with the seat assignment, arrival time, connections – they look at the airline employee for help. And, the agent has no idea what personal concerns that traveler may have. The one action that can make a world of difference for a customer at that moment in time is the simple demonstration of common courtesy.

A genuine smile, a polite tone, the power of "thank you," "please" and "may I" are sometimes all it takes to diffuse an irate, anxious, or frantic customer. Sadly, people are so busy these days, they are often shocked when people express these common courtesies.

You show respect to your customers by truly listening when they speak, tuning out all distractions to ensure you understand what is being said. It's valuing their opinion and carefully considering everything they say, rather than disregarding it quickly with a standard answer. You may have heard the customer's question a thousand times before. But, for your customer, it's the one time they ask the question that is the most important for them.

"Friendly makes sales – and friendly generates repeat business."
Jeffrey Gitomer, author

Execute the Tried-and-True Process

Because the Process Works

The tried-and-true customer service process is all about building relationships one step at a time. When you know what is important to your customers and align your service to meet their needs, what you are selling and supporting becomes valuable. Remember, it's always about your customers' needs, and the benefits your products or services offer to them. It's not about you. So, really get to know your customers; it's an investment that pays great dividends.

What is it that makes your customers successful and how can you support their goals? What are their needs, and how can you meet them? What are their frustrations, and how can you address them? What are their expectations and how can you exceed them? Once you identify the needs, you can provide ultimate customer service.

That's the customer service process, and it really comes in handy when you get in a jam. A great system, with flexibility built in, works. Have respect for the process, use it to your advantage, and do not skip any step in relationship building:

1. Build rapport
2. Listen
3. Assess
4. Respond and resolve
5. Show appreciation

This relationship building process works in any customer situation, and sometimes, like in the situation between Ron and Maria at Nordstrom, Ron covered every step in just three minutes.

Build rapport – Ron noticed Maria coming through the aisle, and walked up to greet her.

Listen – Ron listened with his eyes, observing Maria's demeanor, facial expression, and walking pace.

Assess – He quickly assessed the situation and determined that a return of merchandise was on deck.

Respond and resolve – Ron simply stated, "Would you like me to give you another pair of shoes or would you like a refund?" as he reached for the box of shoes. He handled the credit quickly. He went one step further – a little pizazz – by giving Maria a free merchandise coupon.

Show appreciation – And he closed the interaction, "Thank you for letting me help you today, Maria. It's always my pleasure to help you."

If you're solving a complex technical problem, this process could take several minutes; it may even extend two or three days before the final resolution is at hand. When you have these fundamentals completely embedded into your DNA, they will serve you well throughout the full life cycle of the customer relationship, in brief encounters, in good times, and when things go wrong.

"Customer service is just a day in, day out ongoing, never ending, unremitting, persevering, compassionate, type of activity."
Leon Gorman, Chairman Emeritus, L.L.Bean

▶ *Servicetopia Insight*

> Price is not the main reason for customer churn, it is actually due to the overall poor quality of customer service.[19]

1. Build rapport

Every contact with a customer is a relationship building opportunity, and it starts by building rapport. Lay the ground work for Servicetopia – and establish your own service legacy – by connecting with customers from the very first point of contact. Simply being friendly is a great place to start.

Be interested. Customers are people, not transaction opportunities. There is a life behind every customer and that initial connection is strengthened when you show interest in them as individuals. Ask questions. Discover their likes, activities, and family information. Just taking an interest in their weekend activities opens up casual conversations that will make the working relationship much more pleasant.

Be understanding. Don't just ask questions because it was listed as a technique in your service training. Listen for their answers and respond accordingly. These conversations may take a little more time, but if you want to build rapport, you have to be sincere in your efforts to connect with your customers. Listen to what they say, follow up with additional questions to ensure you truly understand what is being said.

Be trustworthy. In a customer service situation, trust is an essential component of the business-customer relationship. But before a customer will trust you, you must demonstrate trustworthiness. A customer approaches you because of a need for your product or service. You commit to help and you stand by that commitment. Trustworthiness is strengthened with every promise made and promise kept. If the customer needs an answer to a question, you get it. If the customer needs an explanation, you provide it. If a customer needs a demonstration, you arrange it. It's that simple, and it's that important.

"Friends are those rare people who ask how we are and then wait to hear the answer."
Ed Cunningham, American sports announcer and film producer

▶ Servicetopia Insight

What goes into a happy customer experience?
- 78% of customers say: Competent service reps
- 38% of customers say: Personalization [20]

2. Listen

The purpose of listening is to understand. Listening gives you the insight into the full customer situation you need so that you can accurately assess the need and respond with the best product, service, or problem solution. Listening to your customers is also an act of courtesy and a show of respect.

When a customer reaches out to you for your attention, your goal is to carefully tune in for clues as to the nature of the conversation. As you work on your listening skills, it may be helpful to understand why the listening process so often breaks down. Consider these four common barriers to effective listening and develop strategies for eliminating them from your customer interactions.

Preoccupation. We have a lot on our minds. Often when conversing with a customer we are more focused on our own thoughts than what is actually entering our ears. In fact, the American Psychological Association reports that during meetings, 68% of the participants are thinking about events in their lives unrelated to the meeting, 20% of the participants are actually paying attention, and only 12% are really listening. It's discourteous and disrespectful of your customer not to be 100% engaged in the conversation.

Distractions. Noisy environments make it difficult to isolate what the customer says from all the other signals vying for our attention. Even if there are no other sounds, hot, stuffy rooms, visual clutter and other discomforts make it difficult to concentrate on what's being said.

Boredom. Monotone speech patterns, long, seemingly pointless stories that fail to inspire or excite make it incredibly difficult to stay focused on what could be a sticking point for your customer.

Jumping to conclusions. If you assess the point too quickly thinking you've "heard it all before," you tend to just wait your turn to speak and miss critical details of what is important to your customer. Bottom line, don't read your customer's mind.

Ask yourself

- How do you know if you are just hearing your customer and not listening?

- Do you actively listen when the customer was speaking?

- After the conversation, do you remember the key points of what was said?

- Did anything in the conversation confirm or change your actions regarding next steps with this customer?

- Did you learn anything about this customer you didn't know before?

- During the conversation did you find yourself drifting off in your thoughts?

"Customers don't expect you to be perfect. They do expect you to fix things when they go wrong."
Donald Porter, *Vice President, British Airways*

► **Servicetopia Insight**

According to consumers, customer service agents failed to answer their questions 50% of the time. [21]

3. Assess

Some customers will be very precise in the description of their needs or quite specific about the services they want to purchase or defining the problem they may have encountered. However, some customers will be vague or uncertain as to the true nature of their concerns and will have a difficult time getting to the heart of the matter. Sometimes they just aren't sure what they want. Henry Ford once said, "If I gave people what they wanted, I would have given them a faster horse."

That practicality makes your job of listening to understand and assessing to serve that much more important to the process. Think of the assessment stage as a funnel. You start with very broad questions and narrow the conversation down to the heart of the matter upon which both you and the customer agree is the primary objective of the customer interaction.

Assessing the true nature of what customers want to accomplish requires that you actively listen and direct the conversation toward solid conclusions regarding the shape your service needs to take. If you listen long enough, the customer will actually tell you exactly what they want or need. They might even tell you the right solution.

Be careful about trying to read their mind or jump to any conclusions prematurely. Make sure you fully engage your mind and not just your ears. Your ears capture what is said. Your mind assesses what is needed and leads to the best service experience for your customer.

4. Respond and resolve

The goal in customer service is always the same: give the customer the service they want and expect, resolve the customer's problems or issues, and excite them with the result. What can make this goal challenging is the fact that customer interactions are like fingerprints — no two are the same. When you follow the customer service process, however, using all your well-honed skills, you'll wind up at the end game, a successful interaction and a satisfied, loyal customer.

In the previous steps of the customer service process, most of what you do is listen to understand your customers' needs. However, you reach a point when the conversation shifts and you need to respond to what you've heard and understood. This turning point in the conversation accomplishes two purposes: it alerts the customer that you understand the situation and are going to meet that need, and it is a definitive point where your role in the conversation shifts from listener to responder.

That can be very quick, as it was in Ron and Maria's interaction. If it's a cup of coffee your customer wants, you may have suggested a new beverage along the way. But when it comes down to taking the customer order, you will respond with their exact request and verify that you have the order right. If you didn't listen closely, you may miss that extra little pump of mocha.

If it's a technical problem, you could have been working through a troubleshooting process for several minutes. Ultimately, you need to offer the correct solution with confidence or communicate the appropriate expectations for when the problem will be resolved.

The transition to the next step in the process can pivot on a sentence as simple as these examples:

"Here's what I think we should do moving forward…"

"Let's talk about what will work in your situation…"

"As I see it, there are several options here…"

"The single most important thing to remember about any enterprise is that there are no results inside its walls. The result of a business is a satisfied customer."
Peter Drucker, American educator and author

5. Show appreciation

Be sure to show appreciation for your customer and remember to say thank you. Always end on a positive note. When it's your turn to work with a customer, your goal should be not only to take them through the customer service process successfully, but to end on a positive note for the next person who will serve that customer. Picture a graph that rates each service transaction a customer has with your company. The line on the chart rises or falls depending on the rating from one service professional to the next.

Suppose you are the next service agent a customer deals with following a very negative experience from the previous encounter, hoping that the customer even returns for more. How much more difficult will your job be to unravel all the frustrations from the previous interaction?

Ideally, the graph looks like one straight line across the top of the chart, indicating seamless consistency throughout the customer relationship life cycle. Such a consistent level of service builds on your company's reputation for service excellence and invites customers back for quality service every time.

How do you do this?

- Follow the customer service process carefully, and don't skip any points.

- Commit to delivering the best possible service with every customer contact.

- Don't leave any issues unresolved for the next person to deal with. That one unresolved issue could be the reason for a customer defection.

- Ensure the customer is completely satisfied before the conversation ends.

"Customer service shouldn't just be a department, it should be the entire company,"
Tony Hsieh, CEO, Zappos

 @Culturetopia
Process is the key to a consistent customer experience. #Servicetopia

Servicetopia

6.

PIZAZZ

I surprise my customers and everyone feels great!

Seize the Opportunity

Let's have some fun

Pizazz. What is it? You know when you experience it from someone else. You just feel great, and you tell your friends all about it. You know you've added a little pizazz when your customer grins from ear to ear when they wrap up their interaction with you. You know when a customer keeps requesting you to serve them, not anyone else, that you've left a lasting impression – a good lasting impression.

Pizazz is the point when you know you have achieved Servicetopia. You begin with a purpose. You feel the passion. You practice all the principles of professionalism. You follow the process. And, the customer thinks the interaction is complete. But, then you add a little pizazz on top.

Let's have some fun with this! Pizazz is that extra special finishing touch. The cherry on top. The crème de la crème. The gold at the end of the rainbow. A breath of fresh air. Make up a phrase of your own, and make it your own personal statement of pizazz.

Turn negatives into positives

Some of the very best moments when pizazz can make the biggest difference are during those unfortunate situations when your service breaks down, when a customer walks away with a grimace, hangs up the phone in disgust, abandons an online chat session saying "that didn't solve my problem." You may have heard – and taken – the advice not to go to bed angry with your significant other. Take heed. Don't let your customer get away angry.

Good processes help you out in these situations, too. But, go one step further. Treat any problem that arises as an opportunity for you to personally do great things for the customer. Focus on the behavior you display with a customer: act quickly, be fair, apologize, resolve, don't let it happen again, and follow up. Seize the opportunity to use your pizazz and turn negatives into positives.

- **Act quickly** – Customers become impatient when the response is sluggish. The longer the delay the more difficult it will be to achieve satisfaction.

- **Be fair** – In the customer's mind an injustice has occurred. Make sure your recovery efforts are consistent with their sense of justice, not yours.

- **Apologize and resolve the situation** – Sometimes it's tough to admit you made a mistake; yet customers know when mistakes are made. They want the satisfaction that you have acknowledged the mistake, that you're willing to admit it, that the customer was right. Then, most critical of all, fix the situation on the spot.

- **Don't let it happen again** – In most service recovery

efforts, customers will forgive you; but they also want reassurance that the situation won't happen again. Is it a process error? An employee error? A product defect? Be sure to report the problem to the appropriate stakeholders so they can fix the situation to assure that it won't happen again.

- **Follow up** – Let the customer know how you addressed the problem. This extra step, with a little pizazz, goes a long way to repair confidence and reinstill trust.

"We see our customers as invited guests to a party, and we are the hosts. It's our job every day to make every important aspect of the customer experience a little bit better."
Jeff Bezos, CEO Amazon.com

@Culturetopia
When things go wrong, fix it quickly & turn negatives into positives #Servicetopia

Surprise your customer

The people who give the best service, don't do what other companies do better, they do what other companies aren't willing to do. Let that thought settle in for a moment.

How often have you taken someone out for dinner on their birthday and then rushed back to work the next day to enthusiastically tell your co-workers that the restaurant you visited served you dinner quickly and charged you correctly for the meal? Never, right?! That's not a very exciting story. Besides, if you spent $75 to $100 for a nice dinner, would you expect anything less?

But what if, on this occasion, you were escorted to a private candle-lit room where a stringed quartet played soft music and a classically trained vocalist sang "Happy Birthday" as the maître d' presented an elegant birthday cake—all for no extra charge. Before the evening is over, the waiter takes a photograph and as you are walking out the door, the owner greets you with the framed picture taken by the waiter, signed with a personal message to the birthday guest. Think you might tell that story at work? What's the difference? Pizazz—that extra step that surprises and delights your customers beyond their expectations.

Exceeding expectations is a good thing. Surprising, perhaps even shocking your customers with hugely friendly, highly competent, and a seriously fun approach to service is even better. The more you do it, the more it becomes a part of who you are. It becomes your service legacy. And there's a very positive, psychological benefit of surprise – you are getting rewarded for it because everybody just feels better.

Adding pizazz to your efforts will always set you apart from your competition. When you are passionate about service and look for ways to add pizazz in all customer interactions, you ignite those brand evangelists who will gladly carry the torch for your business.

Ask yourself

- What am I willing to start doing now – something I'm not currently doing – to give my customer's a little pizazz?

- Do I create value in every customer interaction?

- How can I go beyond the ordinary to create stories that will be shared with friends and associates?

@Culturetopia
Identify behaviors you can use to surprise your
customers, then deliver with pizazz #Servicetopia

Show empathy

There are some professions whose customers will just naturally pull on your heart strings. If you work at a children's hospital, an oncology ward, a homeless shelter, a refuge for battered women and children, or various social services agencies where the pain of human needs is deeply felt, it isn't too difficult to feel deep empathy.

Regardless of the business environment or customer service location, there is a story behind every customer you serve. Their story might not involve deep human suffering as in the situations above, but every story will involve some level of human drama, and when you learn to empathize with your customers it adds a whole new dimension to your capacity to provide ultimate customer service – to deliver Servicetopia.

Take Starbucks leaders, for example. They explain to their morning crew baristas that they are often the first people their customers will make contact with at the beginning of their day. Each morning, the barista has the opportunity to contribute a positive start for the customer that might offset what could be a challenging and difficult morning. A little pizazz goes a long way in a rushed morning when someone is getting that first cup of coffee or chai tea.

A sales person in a clothing store might be helping someone who has been unemployed for months and is shopping for new clothes for an upcoming round of interviews. An auto mechanic could be diagnosing a problem with a customer's only means of transportation that is essential to their job security.

Put yourself in your customers' shoes. Try to get a sense of their needs and frustrations. Without getting too personal or going beyond the bounds of what is appropriate, get to know your customers' needs and a sense of the world they live in. Express understanding of their situation and take actions to show that you truly empathize with their moment with you.

"The more you engage with customers the clearer things become and the easier it is to determine what you should be doing."
John Russell, President, Harley Davidson

▶ **Servicetopia Insight**

68% of customers quit because of an attitude of indifference towards the customer by the staff. [22]

Show appreciation

It's easy to forget that customers are the reason your business exists. They pay your personal wages and benefits, and without them, you would have no business at all. It's important to keep this front-of-mind so you remember to express appreciation for your customers regularly and consistently. As obvious as this seems, in the midst of the transaction, it's easy to forget to say thank you.

How do you say thank you to your customers? It starts with the simple, genuinely expressed,

"Thank you for your business."

"I really appreciate your business."

"Thank you for the opportunity to work with you."

And with a little pizzaz: "It was my pleasure to serve you!"

Ask yourself

- How can I put Servicetopia on auto-pilot?

Consider this

The next time your team assembles for a meeting, consider brainstorming creative ways to express appreciation to your customers.

- What actions do people take that make you feel special and appreciated?

- What can we do that we have never done before to express appreciation to our customers?

- What might be the least expected way to show customers we appreciate them?

- How can we show appreciation to our customers in a genuine way without spending any money?

- If money were no object, how could we surprise our customers with appreciation?

- Now how can we achieve those "pizzazzy" ideas within our budget restrictions?

"Gratitude is not only the greatest of virtues, but the parent of all others."
Cicero, Roman philosopher

@Culturetopia
Create value and show appreciation for every customer with every experience. #Servicetopia

Pay It Forward

We met Johnny Bagger when we began our journey to Servicetopia. Remember the small pieces of paper with big messages handwritten on them? Remember the customers who would wait in line a little longer just to see Johnny and their inspiration for the day? Remember the deli clerk who Johnny inspired to put Snoopy stickers on the wrapped packages and the florist to hand out flower blossoms to unexpecting shoppers? Everyone is inspired. Everyone feels great. And all it takes is a little pizazz. Pay it forward.

@Culturetopia
Leave a legacy of #Servicetopia where everyone feels great. Celebrate.

Spread the Inspiration

Servicetopia sounds like perfection, and it might be. But, we can aspire to it; we can practice the fine art, we can achieve it, and we can pay it forward into the hearts and minds of other service providers. You've read about Servicetopia now. But, the value of a book is completely dependent on the degree to which it influences your attitudes and actions. It's time to take action. Make someone's day. Share some of your "ahas." Go for it.

Here are some ideas on ways to share Servicetopia:

Partner with other employees in your company and form a weekly discussion group to elaborate on the application of customer service principles within your company and use the questions throughout the book as your guide.

Use the chapters as meeting starters to uphold the priority of customer service excellence throughout your company.

Share what you learn from the book in brainstorming or problem solving discussions or during meetings when the principles relate to the topic under discussion.

Observe how these principles are demonstrated – or violate – when you become the customer at another place of business. Give them your candid feedback and bring that experience back to your team.

Use some of the key points in presentations you are asked to give in upcoming meetings as a way of promoting the importance of customer service.

Special Thanks

I would like to thank everyone that has been a part of making this book possible. Like any worthwhile endeavor, it takes a group of dedicated individuals, working as a team to realize success.

Thank you to the many front-line service professionals I've observed over the years that have demonstrated Servicetopia and inspire me to encourage others to do the same.

Thank you to John Manning for helping me put to words the foundational ideas and principles of Servicetopia.

Thank you to Cinda Daly for her tireless work on editing and further developing the concepts contained in this book.

Thank you to Kurt Baxter for helping publish the book and getting it in the hands of many readers.

And thank you to you, the reader, for taking the time to read this book. You make all the effort worthwhile!

Aloha!

Jason Young

Jason Young has been called a "rare breed" when it comes to developing leaders and customer service initiatives. As a former senior-level manager at Southwest Airlines, Jason learned the value of a successful workplace culture. During his 10 years of service the airline consistently rated No. 1 in customer service and employee satisfaction,  he was a key driver in creating and developing the company's innovative training programs for the successful leadership and customer service culture that has become renowned in the business world today.

Driven by the need to extend his unique insight in leadership development to others outside Southwest, Jason separated from the pack in 1998 to launch his own consulting practice.

Today, as president of LeadSmart, Inc., Jason shares his vision in developing successful corporate cultures and workplace environments and creating exemplary customer service. He works with forward-thinking companies, including Starbucks, Ericsson, Coca Cola and Tyson Foods, to name just a few. He has even returned to his old turf – Southwest Airlines – to extend his knowledge as a corporate training consultant in leadership development area once again.

Jason captured his philosophy of creating high performance cultures in his popular book, *The Culturetopia Effect* and extends the fine art of exemplary customer service in his newest book, *Servicetopia*.

Invite Jason to Speak

Jason Young's keynote presentations and training programs are in demand for audiences of all types – from senior level executives to front line employees. Jason's messages reach to the core of every audience member with his unique style and engaging presentation skills. Participants are treated to a compelling experience that will change the way they view themselves, their customers and the company for which they work. The result is an inspirational encounter that resonates long after his presentation is over.

Jason is an expert at integrating your meeting objectives into powerful and compelling presentations that touch the heart and motivate any audience! Invite Jason to be your next keynote speaker. Ask him to be your trusted advisor as you bring Servicetopia into your organization. Have him bring his team of workshop facilitators – professionals who practice and deliver Servicetopia every day – to guide your organization through the "Servicetopia Experience."

Jason's popular presentations include:

Culturetopia - The Ultimate High Performance Workplace

Servicetopia - The Ultimate Customer Service Experience

The Southwest Way - Practices of a Market Leader

Lead Smart - High Performance Leadership

The New Diversity - The Generational Workforce

For more info on training and keynotes by Jason Young

www.culturetopia.com

Footnote References

1: ContactPoint Client Research and Ruby Newell-Legner, Founder, 7 Star Service

2: SHRM Employee Job Satisfaction and Engagement Survey, 2012

3: McKinsey, 20 Important Customer Experience Facts for 2014, as published by Adlib Software, August, 2013.

4: Convergys Customer Scorecard Research, 2013

5: Global Customer Service Barometer, Echo Research, on behalf of American Express, 2012

6: Source: Brad Tuttle, Customer Service Hell, Time, 2011

7: Emmet Murphy, Mark Murphy, Leading on the Edge of Chaos: The 10 Critical Elements for Success in Volatile Times, Prentice Hall Press, 2002

8: Employee Engagement: Maximizing Organizational Performance, Right Management, 2013

9: Harvard University Research

10: Gallup Employee Engagement Survey, 2012

11: Accenture Global Consumer Pulse Survey, 2013

12: Source: Customer Service Experience Impact Report, Harris Interactive/RightNow 2011

13: Source: Pew Research Center's Internet and American Life Project, 2010

14: Source: "Understanding Customers," Ruby Newell-Legner, Founder 7 Star Service

15: Source: Convergys Customer Scorecard Research, 2013

16: Source: Zogby Analytics, 24/7 Wall St

17: Albert Mehrabian, Silent Messages: Implicit Communication of Emotions and Attitudes, Wadsworth, 1971

18: Accenture Global Customer Satisfaction Report, 2008

19: Genesys Global Survey, The Cost of Poor Customer Service, 2009

20: Harris Interactive

21: Harris Interactive

22: Michael Leboeuf, How To Win Customers and Keep Them for Life, Berkley Trade, 2000